T0398229

Welcome to Iceland

By Ben Hubbard

DK | Penguin Random House

Senior Editors Carrie Love, Shannon Beatty
Assistant Editor Gunjan Mewati
Senior Art Editor Rachael Parfitt
Art Editor Bhagyashree Nayak
Assistant Art Editor Simran Lakhiani
Jacket Coordinator Issy Walsh
Jacket Designer Dheeraj Arora
DTP Designers Vikram Singh, Sachin Gupta
Picture Researchers Rituraj Singh, Sumedha Chopra
Production Editor Abi Maxwell
Production Controller John Casey
Managing Editors Penny Smith, Monica Saigal
Managing Art Editor Ivy Sengupta
Delhi Creative Heads Glenda Fernandes, Malavika Talukder
Publishing Manager Francesca Young
Deputy Art Director Mabel Chan
Publishing Director Sarah Larter

Reading Consultant Dr. Barbara Marinak
Subject Consultant Angus Konstam

First American Edition, 2021
Published in the United States by DK Publishing
1450 Broadway, Suite 801, New York, NY 10018

Copyright © 2021 Dorling Kindersley Limited
DK, a Division of Penguin Random House LLC
21 22 23 24 25 10 9 8 7 6 5 4 3 2 1
001–321629–Dec/2021

A catalog record for this book is available from the Library of Congress.
ISBN: 978-0-7440-2712-9 (Paperback)
ISBN: 978-0-7440-2713-6 (Hardcover)

DK books are available at special discounts when purchased
in bulk for sales promotions, premiums, fund-raising, or
educational use. For details, contact: DK Publishing Special Markets,
1450 Broadway, Suite 801, New York, NY 10018
SpecialSales@dk.com

Printed and bound in China

The publisher would like to thank the following for their kind permission to reproduce their photographs:
(Key: a-above; b-below/bottom; c-center; f-far; l-left; r-right; t-top)
1 Alamy Stock Photo: Juniors Bildarchiv GmbH (b). **5 Getty Images / iStock:** patpongs. **6-7 Dreamstime.com:**
Jon Helgason (b). **7 Alamy Stock Photo:** Arterra Picture Library (c). **8 Getty Images / iStock:** DieterMeyrl.
9 Alamy Stock Photo: Peter Barritt. **10-11 Alamy Stock Photo:** Juniors Bildarchiv GmbH. **12 Dreamstime.com:**
Henkbogaard (t). **Getty Images / iStock:** Mizuki Kato (b). **13 Dreamstime.com:** Lecock Freddy. **14 Dreamstime.com:**
Peter Hermes Furian (t). **14-15 Shutterstock.com:** SAPhotog (t). **16 Dreamstime.com:** Mypointofview (cb).
Getty Images / iStock: pedrojperez (br). **17 Getty Images / iStock:** Snorri Guðmundsson (c). **18 Dreamstime.com:**
Artofphoto. **19 Getty Images:** Simon Hofmann / Bongarts. **20-21 Dreamstime.com:** Tawatchai Prakobkit.
22 Dreamstime.com: Tawatchai Prakobkit (bl); Pytyczech (tl); Tampaci (cla); Robin Runck (cl).
Getty Images: Simon Hofmann / Bongarts (clb).

Cover images: *Front:* **Dreamstime.com:** Suranga Weeratunga; *Back:* **Dreamstime.com:** Marek Rybar tl.

Endpaper images: *Front:* **Dreamstime.com:** Sandy Matzen; *Back:* **Dreamstime.com:** Sandy Matzen.

All other images © Dorling Kindersley
For further information see: www.dkimages.com

For the curious
www.dk.com

MIX
Paper from
responsible sources
FSC™ C018179

This book was made with Forest
Stewardship Council™ certified paper—
one small step in DK's commitment to
a sustainable future. For more information
go to www.dk.com/our-green-pledge

Contents

Where is Iceland?

Iceland is a country in Europe.
It is an island in the Atlantic Ocean.
The capital city is Reykjavik (RAKE-ya-veek).

4

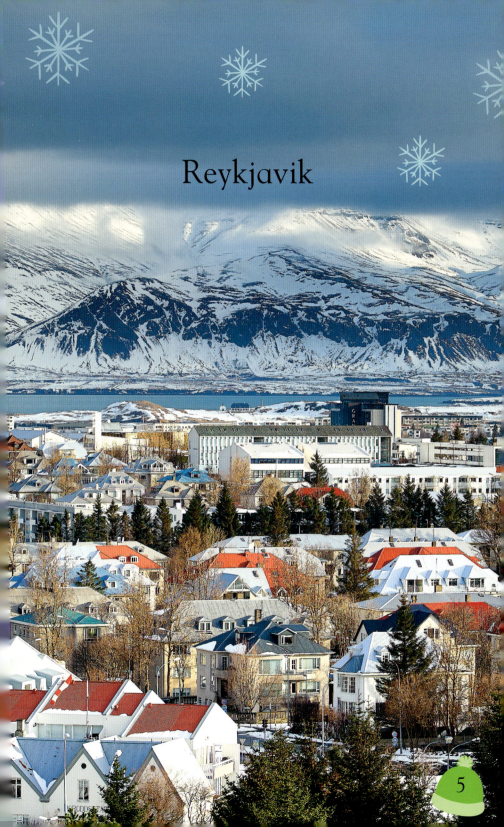

Reykjavik

Fire and ice

An ice cap is a
thick mass of snow.
Areas of Iceland are
covered by ice caps.

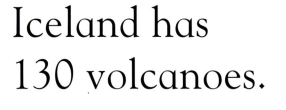

Iceland has 130 volcanoes.

Hot springs

Iceland is covered
in natural hot springs.
The water is heated
by hot rocks.
People swim in the springs.

Blue Lagoon

Icelandic horses

The Icelandic horse is small and strong.

It has a thick coat to stay warm in the snow.

Puffins

The puffin is a small seabird.
It can fly and swim.
There are almost 10 million
puffins in Iceland.

Puffin
chick

Vikings

The Vikings discovered Iceland. They settled there over 1,000 years ago.

Viking
longhouse

They lived together
in longhouses.

Food

People eat lamb soup, hotdogs, and shark meat.

Lamb soup

Hotdog

Skyr

They eat yogurt for dessert.
It's called skyr (s-KEER).

Sports

People climb mountains
in Iceland.
Handball is popular too.

Northern lights

You can see the northern lights in Iceland.

These are natural lights
in the sky.

Glossary

Europe
continent with
over 50 countries

handball
sport played by two
teams using a small ball

hot spring
pool of warm water that
is heated by hot rocks

ice cap
thick mass of
ice and snow

Northern lights
natural light display
seen near the Arctic

Index

23

A LEVEL FOR EVERY READER

This book is a part of an exciting four-level reading series to support
children in developing the habit of reading widely for both pleasure
and information. Each book is designed to develop a child's reading skills,
fluency, grammar awareness, and comprehension in order to
build confidence and enjoyment when reading.

Ready for a Level 1 (Learning to Read) book

A child should:

- be familiar with most letters and sounds.
- understand how to blend sounds together to make words.
- have an awareness of syllables and rhyming sounds.

A valuable and shared reading experience

For many children, learning to read requires much effort, but adult
participation can make reading both fun and easier. Here are a few tips
on how to use this book with an early reader:

Check out the contents together:

- tell the child the book title and talk about what the book might be about.
- read about the book on the back cover and talk about the contents page
  to help heighten interest and expectation.
- chat about the pictures on each page.
- discuss new or difficult words.

Support the reader:

- give the book to the young reader to turn the pages.
- if the book seems too hard, support the child by sharing the reading task.

Talk at the end of each page:

- ask questions about the text and the meaning of the words used—this helps
  develop comprehension skills.

Reading consultant: Dr. Barbara Marinak, Dean and Professor of Education at
Mount St. Mary's University, Maryland.